In Reverse

Nicole Harvey

Presentation by *BookLeaf Publishing*

Web: www.bookleafpub.com

E-mail: info@bookleafpub.com

ISBN: 9789357614092

First edition 2022

Death

Down in the ground you'll find my roots
Earth provides all of my fruits
After I break the mould
The wind carries gold
Higher than past pursuits

Community

A smile
A wave
A high five
Unwavering support
Regardless of your ability
An old friend
A new friend
A stranger

Betrayal

Once they were a formidable pair
Spending each waking moment hand in hand.
They made themselves a mighty lair
In which they planned to make a stand.

It was an easy plan to plot
Take over the world, we will.
Before we get caught
We'll make a mill.

Yet 'twas not to be
This mighty team
Because what became of them you'll see
 Was a collapse of their dastardly scheme.

All it takes is an actor's portrayal
And one is left with an infinite betrayal.

Golden Shovel of Neen Cohen

I'll always be there
To fulfill your needs
Ends of the earth un-to
Your rock I'll be
Forever more
A love so beautiful
Eyes of tears

Blood/Water

5

They are there
They are here
They're in your heart
They're in your soul

Some you're born to
Some are born to you
Some are chosen
Some choose you

Blood is thicker than water
Yet everything can be diluted
For if it be poisoned
Best ye sever it off

Waffle 243

She walked around the inlet, sand between her
toes
The sea breeze brushed her ratty hair, the air
salty in her nose.

She rolled up her sleeves, talons at the ready
"I've got your measure, cliff" said she.

Though not catering to her abilities, she knew
she was summit-bound
Once the queen of fancy, now ready to be
recrowned.

RSP

Skinny at the top
All four sides, identical
wide at the bottom

She Walked Out The Door

She walked out the door
Gift sat wrapped upon the bench
A basket of laundry
Half drawn sketch

Bills on the counter
Meat thawing on the sink
Dip in her mattress
Still distinct

Beside the armchair
A book lay open on the floor
That morning she walked
Out the door

Golden Shovel of Daddy by Sylvia Plath

It's time to say goodbye, Daddy.
This which may be a burden, I
Don't see it so. The choice I have,
The choice I made. You had
A new place onward to.
For not your soul I deigned to kill,
Just your mind I took from you.

L.O.V.E.

Live life fully
A lifestyle fit for a king
Of largest heart

Open your mind
Open your soul
Opulence is obvious

Value vulnerability
Avoid vanity
Emerge the victor

Evoke the equilibrium
Passion meld with effort
Eclipse all other emotions

Tired

Tired
Tire
Tir
Ti
T

Zzzz

Eternal

The idea of living without you
is one so foreign
You've been there forever

You give of yourself
To support my life
To protect my heart

The day will come
May it be far off
In the distant future

Combined Golden Shovel of Neen Cohen

As life is close to death
It seems easy to think that the
Heart is what breeds eternal.
The pace maker of our life becomes the
peacemaker.

To live by the heart, views become warped.
A place to get lost in
The ideal becoming patterned
Clear as cracked crystal.

Guilt

Grave mistake, unacceptable
Ill-advised
Lifelong remorse, torment

Sisters

Impart your wisdom
Take my hand
Love has come
Making footprints in dry sand

Dress me like a living doll
Thrash me at monopoly
Support is giving all
Make me eat my broccoli

Hide the chocolate
Give me guidance
Remind me I'm the smallest
Lifelong alliance

Maggie

My new little friend
Nuts become your favourite
I squawk you listen

Shadow

The shadow looms
Overwhelming large
The shadow is a monster
His life is mighty angry
I attempt to turn and see him
But he likes to try to hide
Finally I start to talk
And he begins to listen
The words spill more and more
His anger starts to shrink
He even cracks a smile
The shadow stands beside me
At last, he is a friend.

Regret

Action not taken
Sole regret
Right or wrong
A life long wonder

Listen, watch, sit immobile
A comforting word
Or a gentle hug
A mind that dwells in hindsight

Go

You are the dewdrop on the morning leaf
The cat who spied the mouse
The racecar as the light turns green

You are the wave that hit it's peak
An athlete on the starting block
A shooting star about to fall

You are a raincloud due to burst
A bird leaving its nest
A child atop a slide

Now go

My Crew

You are my one, my two, my three
I met you and found my crew
I met you and my heart grew wide
Pure, rich, love

Wherever you will be
I will always come back to you
I will always be by your side
Today, tomorrow, forever

Life

Light so bright
Is it the devil I'm meeting?
Full of emotion
Everything comes anew